DO...

RECIPES

Compiled by Julia Skinner

THE FRANCIS FRITH COLLECTION

www.francisfrith.com

First published in the United Kingdom in 2011 by The Francis Frith Collection®

This edition published exclusively for Bradwell Books in 2012
For trade enquiries see: www.bradwellbooks.com or tel: 0800 834 920
ISBN 978-1-84589-572-3

British Library Cataloguing in Publication Data

Flavours of Dorset - Recipes
Compiled by Julia Skinner

The Francis Frith Collection
Oakley Business Park,
Wylye Road, Dinton,
Wiltshire SP3 5EU
Tel: +44 (0) 1722 716 376
Email: info@francisfrith.co.uk
www.francisfrith.com

Printed and bound in Malaysia
Contains material sourced from responsibly managed forests

Front Cover: **EYPE, JESSAMINE COTTAGE 1897** 40089p
Frontispiece: **CHILD OKEFORD, THE CROSS 1900** C222001

The colour-tinting is for illustrative purposes only, and is not intended to be historically accurate

AS WITH ANY HISTORICAL DATABASE, THE FRANCIS FRITH ARCHIVE IS CONSTANTLY BEING
CORRECTED AND IMPROVED, AND THE PUBLISHERS WOULD WELCOME INFORMATION ON
OMISSIONS OR INACCURACIES

CONTENTS

INTRODUCTION

'If you in Do'set be a-roamen,
An' ha' business at a farm
Then won't ye zee your eale a-foamen!
Or your cider down to warm?
Woon't ye have brown bread a-put ye?
An' some vinney cheese a-cut ye?
Butter? Rolls o't!
Cream? Why bowls o't!'

Not a lot has changed since Reverend William Barnes (1801-86) wrote these words in the Dorset dialect in his poem 'In Praise of Dorset' in the 19th century. Dorset is still famous for its food, although nowadays the excellent lamb, beef, and pork produced on Dorset farms as well as venison and other wild game, soft fruit and vegetables, watercress, fantastic cheeses, dairy products, ice-cream, preserves, chutneys, baked goods, a wealth of wonderful fish and shellfish and even chillies and olives would be added to the list, to mention just a few of the delicious things you can find. Dorset produce is available at regular farmers' markets in most towns of the county, as well as from farm shops, street markets, good butchers and many shops in towns and villages that take great pride in selling high quality produce from local suppliers. Dorset showcases its food in a number of food festivals around the county each year, and an annual Cheese Festival is held in Sturminster Newton in north Dorset. And there is still plenty of cream to be had in this beautiful county, either to spread on a scone in a Dorset cream tea, or to accompany a warm slice of that iconic delicacy, Dorset Apple Cake, fresh from the oven.

Flavours of ...
DORSET
RECIPES

CHIDEOCK, GATHERING THE HAY 1922 72803

RECIPE

NETTLE SOUP

One of England's most eccentric events takes place in Dorset each June, when the annual Stinging Nettle Eating Championship is held at the Bottle Inn at Marshwood, north-east of Lyme Regis – the brave competitors who take part actually eat raw nettles! However, the shoots of young nettles have been cooked and eaten in the early spring by country people for centuries as a welcome and nutritious source of fresh greens. Only the tender top sprigs should be picked (wearing gloves!) and eaten, and can be cooked in the same way as spinach, or made into a tasty soup, as given here. The acid which causes the nettles to sting is destroyed by cooking. For a variation, try mixing some watercress or Cos lettuce leaves with the nettles, or a few fresh or frozen peas. It is also good if you add 2-3 de-rinded rashers of bacon into the pan with the potato and onion, chopped into small pieces.

> 1 large onion, peeled and chopped
> 1 garlic clove, crushed or finely chopped
> 450g/1 lb potatoes, peeled and diced into small pieces
> 225g/8oz young nettle tops or young leaves
> 50g/2oz butter
> 1 litre/1¾ pints good chicken or vegetable stock
> Salt and freshly ground black pepper
> Finely chopped fresh parsley or chives, to garnish

Wash and drain the nettles, trim off the leaves and discard the stems and any discoloured leaves. Melt the butter in a large saucepan and sauté the chopped potatoes, onions and garlic until the onion begins to soften and go transparent. Add the nettles to the pan and stir around a bit, then add the stock. Bring to the boil, then reduce the heat, cover the pan and leave to simmer for about 15 minutes, until the potato is soft. Leave to cool for a few minutes, then zap the soup in a blender or liquidizer, return to the pan and season to taste with salt and freshly ground black pepper. Reheat and serve in individual soup bowls with a swirl of cream, yogurt or crème fraiche on top and a garnish of finely chopped fresh parsley or chives.

LYME REGIS, THE OLD FOSSIL SHOP c1891 L121417

RECIPES

SPICY TOMATO, PEPPER AND CHILLI SOUP

Red hot chilli peppers might not seem an obvious product of rural
Dorset, but one of the country's specialist chilli growers is based at
Sea Spring Farm at West Bexington, near Bridport in west Dorset.
They even produce a chilli variety called the Dorset Naga, which is
one of the hottest chillies in the world, with a wonderful aroma and
flavour. Fresh chillies from Sea Spring Farm are in season from August
to November and can be bought online from the farm's website,
www.peppersbypost.biz. This is a quick and easy recipe for a hot,
spicy soup that is ideal for a cold winter's day. It is also delicious eaten
cold as a summer dish, with a teaspoonful of natural yogurt swirled
into each bowl. Use a variety of chilli as hot as you prefer in this soup
– even a Dorset Naga if you dare!

> 225g/8oz red peppers, trimmed, seeded and cut into slices
> 1 onion, peeled and chopped
> 2 garlic cloves, crushed or finely chopped
> 1 fresh chilli, trimmed, deseeded and chopped
> 1 x 400g/14oz tin tomatoes and their juice
> 600ml/1 pint vegetable or chicken stock
> 2 tablespoonfuls chopped fresh basil leaves, to garnish

Put the sliced red peppers in a large saucepan with the chopped
onion, garlic and chillies. Add the tomatoes and stock and bring to
the boil, stirring well. Reduce the heat and gently cook the soup at a
low simmer for 20-30 minutes, until the red peppers have softened.
Remove from the heat and allow the soup to cool a little, then
process it in a blender or liquidizer until smooth and return it to the
pan. When ready to serve, reheat and serve in soup bowls with a
garnish of finely chopped basil leaves.

WATERCRESS SOUP

Dorset is one of the UK's main areas for the production of watercress, especially around Dorchester and Bere Regis. Watercress can be eaten raw as a salad or in sandwiches or used to make a sauce to accompany fish, but is most famous for making a delicious soup. Traditionally-grown watercress is cultivated in flowing watercourses of mineral-rich water of the highest purity, making this a super-food packed with nutrients, with a distinctive peppery, slightly bitter, flavour. Watercress has been eaten in Britain for centuries, but in earlier times it was mainly valued for its medicinal properties. It was only adopted into the general diet in the early 19th century, when it began to be commercially and hygienically produced in large quantities. The virtues of watercress soup were described by Dr Nicholas Culpepper in his 'The Compleat Herbal' of 1653: 'Watercress pottage [soup] is a good remedy to cleanse the blood in the spring, and help headaches, and consume the gross humours winter has left behind; those that would live in health may use it if they please; if they will not, I cannot help it. If any fancy not pottage, they may eat the herb as a salad.'

> 50g/2oz butter
> 2 bunches of watercress with their stalks removed,
>   washed and chopped *(but reserve a few sprigs
>   to garnish the soup)*
> 1 medium onion, chopped
> 25g/1oz plain flour
> 600ml/1 pint milk
> 450ml/ ¾ pint chicken or vegetable stock
> 6 tablespoonfuls single cream

Melt the butter in a large pan, and gently fry the watercress and onion for a few minutes until softened. Stir in the flour and cook for a further one minute. Slowly stir in the milk, a little at a time, and then the stock. Bring to the boil, stirring all the time, until thickened, then cover and simmer gently for 30 minutes. Remove from the heat and cool for a few minutes, then liquidize. Before serving, add the cream and reheat gently, taking care not to allow the soup to boil. Serve with a swirl of cream and a sprig of watercress leaves to garnish.

BRIDPORT, EAST STREET 1930 83342

RECIPE

SALMON STEAKS WITH DILL BUTTER

Christchurch (formerly in Hampshire, but now in east Dorset) is on the estuaries of two rivers, the Avon and the Stour. The Royalty Fishery a few miles from the mouth of the Avon has been famous for its salmon and sea trout since medieval times. A landmark of Christchurch is its beautiful priory. At the top of its west tower is a huge weathervane in the shape of a golden salmon, which was placed there not only as a symbol of Christianity, but also to commemorate the gift of the first salmon of the season to the Prior. This recipe for fresh salmon steaks baked in the oven with herb-flavoured butter is enough for 4 people – increase quantities for more.

> 4 salmon steaks
> 50g/2oz butter, softened to room temperature
> Finely grated rind of half a lemon
> 1 tablespoonful lemon juice
> 1 tablespoonful finely chopped fresh dill
> 2 lemon slices, cut into halves
> 4 sprigs of fresh dill
> Salt and freshly ground black pepper, to taste

Place the butter, lemon rind, lemon juice, chopped dill and salt and pepper in a bowl, and mix it well together with a fork, to make the dill butter. Spoon the butter mixture on to a piece of greaseproof paper and roll it up to form a sausage shape. Wrap in cling film and place in the freezer or ice box of the fridge for 20 minutes, until it is firm. Pre-heat the oven to 190°C/375°F/Gas Mark 5. Cut out four pieces of foil each big enough to encase a salmon steak, grease them lightly and place a salmon steak in the centre of each piece. Unwrap the dill butter and slice it into 8 rounds. Place two rounds of the dill butter on top of each salmon steak with one of the lemon pieces between them, and place a sprig of dill on top. Bring up the edges of the foil to encase each piece of salmon in a foil parcel and crinkle the edges to seal firmly. Place the parcels on a baking sheet and cook in the pre-heated oven for 20-25 minutes. Remove from the oven, undo the foil and slide the salmon steaks with their topping on to warmed serving plates, pour the juices from the parcel on to each salmon steak and serve.

CHRISTCHURCH, THE PRIORY AND THE RIVER 1918
68052A

WEYMOUTH, THE PARADE 1898 41119

A wide variety of fish is caught off the Dorset coast, and fishermen
will often let you buy fish direct from their boats as they come back
to harbour with their catch. The more valuable catches brought
in, such as Dover sole or skate, tend to be sent to London or the
fashionable seafood restaurants in the county, but you can usually
buy the bi-catch, such as plaice, flounders or brill, at a good price.
By buying locally-caught fish rather than frozen imported seafood,
either from the fishing boats or from local fishmongers, you can be
sure that the fish is in its proper season, completely fresh and thus
full of flavour. If you want to catch fresh fish yourself, you can also go
out to sea on fishing trips from most of the seaside resorts like Lyme
Regis, West Bay, Weymouth, Swanage and Poole.

RECIPE

BRILL WITH LEMON AND CAPER SAUCE

Some fish species are now in short supply, but brill is found in good
numbers in Dorset waters. Brill is a very versatile fish with a delicate
flavour. It is similar to turbot in having succulent, slightly sweet flesh,
but with none of the bony tubercles. Brill are very easy to fillet before
or after cooking. They are particularly good when cooked on the
bone, either by grilling, frying or baking. As with any white fish, cook
until the flesh is just opaque, firm to the touch and easy to flake. In
this recipe, brill fillets are served with a zesty dressing that is also
good with skate, plaice and Dover or lemon sole. Serves 4.

    4 fillets of brill
    25g/1oz butter, melted
    Salt and pepper
    For the dressing:
    Juice of 2 lemons
    50g/2oz unsalted butter
    4 teaspoonfuls capers, drained and rinsed
    1 tablespoonful chopped fresh parsley

Pre-heat the grill to hot. Line a grill pan with kitchen foil, and place
it under a grill to pre-warm. Place the fillets (skin side down) on the
warmed foil. Brush the fish with the melted butter and season to
taste with salt and pepper. Cook under a hot grill for 2-8 minutes
depending on the thickness of the fish fillets, without turning them
over, until the fish is cooked as above. When cooked, arrange the fish
on a hot serving dish, and keep warm whilst you make the dressing.

Add 4 tablespoonfuls of water to the lemon juice. Heat the butter in
a heavy-based pan until it is melted and browned, but not scorched.
Add the lemon juice, half at first, then taste the sauce and add the
other half if you want. Add the capers and parsley, and season well to
taste. Pour the dressing over the fish and serve, with vegetables such
as new potatoes and peas, green beans or wilted spinach.

POOLE, THE GUILDHALL 1904 52812

RECIPES

CIDERED COD CASSEROLE

Poole's prosperity for centuries was linked with the Newfoundland cod trade. Hundreds of ships sailed from Poole for Newfoundland each spring, returning with cargoes of salt-dried cod. The Mansion House in Thames Street (now a hotel) was built in the 1770s by the brothers Isaac and Benjamin Lester, who had a large fishing station at Trinity, Newfoundland, and ran the biggest fleet in the trade. They celebrated the object of their success in their home by having two fillets of dried codfish carved in marble on the fireplace of what is now the Lester-Garland room (see below). Cod is still caught by Dorset fishermen, but is expensive because it is now in short supply – if you prefer, use a cheaper fish such as haddock, whiting, or pollack as an alternative to cod in this recipe.

> 450-675g/1-1½ lbs cod fillet, skinned (or alternative fish)
> 225g/8oz fresh tomatoes, skinned and sliced
> 50g/2oz mushrooms, sliced
> 1 tablespoonful finely chopped fresh parsley
> Salt and pepper
> 150ml/ ¼ pint cider
> 2 tablespoonfuls fresh white breadcrumbs
> 50g/2oz grated cheese

Pre-heat the oven to 180ºC/350ºF/Gas Mark 4. Cut the fish into cubes and place in a buttered ovenproof dish. Cover the fish with the sliced tomatoes, mushrooms, and parsley. Season to taste, and pour the cider over. Cover with the dish with foil and bake in the pre-heated oven for 25 minutes. Take the dish out of the oven, remove the foil, and sprinkle over the breadcrumbs and cheese. Place the dish under a hot grill and cook until the cheese has melted and the topping is crisp and browned.

STUFFED MACKEREL WITH GOOSEBERRY SAUCE

Bournemouth (formerly in Hampshire but now in Dorset) did not exist at all until Captain Lewis Tregonwell built a holiday home in the area in 1810-11, in the middle of empty heathland, on the site of what is now the Royal Exeter Hotel. Captain Tregonwell began to develop the area with villas to let out for holidays, others saw the potential and followed suit, and Bournemouth was on the map. Bournemouth is now one of England's most popular holiday destinations, but when Captain Tregonwell built his holiday retreat in the area, his house was the only building, apart from an inn, on a wild stretch of coastline frequented only by turf cutters, smugglers and mackerel fishermen. Mackerel are caught in good numbers all along the Dorset coast, and are delicious. In this recipe, mackerel are served up with a tasty stuffing and a gooseberry sauce – gooseberries have long been a favourite accompaniment to mackerel in West Country cookery. Gooseberry jam also makes a great accompaniment to cold smoked mackerel fillets, served with brown bread and butter. Serves 4.

> 4 mackerel, gutted and de-scaled
> 1 tablespoonful finely chopped parsley
> 1 tablespoonful finely chopped thyme
> Half a teaspoonful grated lemon rind
> 1 tablespoonful lemon juice
> 25g/1oz soft white breadcrumbs
> Enough seasoned plain flour to coat the fish
> 225g/8oz gooseberries
> Sugar to taste

Pre-heat the oven to 180°C/350°F/Gas Mark 4. Wash and dry the mackerel, and clean them. Mix the parsley, thyme, lemon rind, lemon juice and soft breadcrumbs and stuff the mackerel with this mixture. Roll the fish lightly in seasoned flour. Melt a little butter or oil in a baking pan and, when it is very hot, put in the mackerel. Put into the pre-heated oven and bake for 25 minutes, carefully turning the fish over halfway through.

Meanwhile, for the gooseberry sauce, simmer the gooseberries in very little water until they are soft. Rub them through a sieve and sweeten lightly. Warm the gooseberry sauce through before serving with the mackerel.

flavours of ...
DORSET
FISH

BOURNEMOUTH, THE PIER 1897 40559

FRAMPTON, THE VILLAGE 1906 54584

The recipe on the opposite page is an old way of slow-cooking beef in a richly flavoured gravy. It can be left to cook for as long as necessary, but the forcemeat (sausagemeat) balls should not be cooked for too long. 'Jugging' was an easy way of stewing meat in homes without an oven in the past; the meat was put into a jug, or 'pipkin', with a lid, with liquid and herbs, and then the container was stood in a pan of boiling water and cooked for several hours, with the water in the container being topped up from time to time. This method cooked the meat slowly in the liquid until it was very tender, allowing the meat to retain its flavour whilst it mingled with that of the other ingredients it was cooked with. Nowadays, this dish can be cooked in a casserole dish in the oven instead, and it will make your kitchen smell delicious!

RECIPE

DORSET JUGGED STEAK WITH FORCEMEAT BALLS

The addition of the forcemeat (sausagemeat) balls to this dish was a way of making the meat go further to feed a large family, and makes this a very filling dish; you can omit them if you wish, and just make the meat stew – if you do this, remove the casserole lid for the final 20 minutes of the cooking time, to thicken up the sauce. Serves 4.

675g/1½ lbs stewing beef (shin of beef gives the best flavour)
25g/1oz plain flour, seasoned with salt and pepper
1 tablespoonful cooking oil
1 onion, peeled and left whole
4 cloves
150ml/ ¼ pint port or red wine
450ml/ ¾ pint beef stock
1 teaspoonful mixed dried herbs
Salt and pepper
1 tablespoonful redcurrant jelly
115g/4oz sausagemeat
115g/4oz fresh breadcrumbs
1 egg, beaten
2 tablespoonfuls finely chopped fresh parsley

Pre-heat the oven to 160°C/300°F/Gas Mark 3. Cut the meat into cubes and toss in the seasoned flour. Heat the oil in a large frying pan and gently fry the meat in batches for a few minutes, turning the cubes over so that all sides are lightly browned. Put the meat in a casserole dish. Stud the onion with the cloves and add to the dish, then pour in the port, or red wine, and enough of the stock to cover the meat, reserving the rest. Add the mixed herbs, season to taste and stir well. Cover the dish with its lid and cook in the pre-heated oven for 2-2½ hours, until the meat is tender. Check the dish occasionally to make sure that the liquid has not run dry – top up with the reserved stock, or some water, if necessary. About 30 minutes before the dish is ready to serve, stir the redcurrant jelly into the casserole. Then prepare the forcemeat balls. Mix together the sausagemeat, breadcrumbs, beaten egg and parsley, and season to taste. Flour your hands and form the mixture into small balls. Poach the balls in boiling water for 10 minutes, then drain them and add to the casserole. Remove the casserole lid and cook for a further 15 minutes, uncovered, until the forcemeat balls are cooked and slightly brown.

RECIPE

DORSET LAMB WITH HONEY AND CIDER GLAZE

Dorset has been famous for the quality of its mutton and lamb for centuries. In past times mutton from the Portland breed was especially celebrated, and although this is now a rare breed, quality lamb is still produced on Dorset farms. This recipe gives a spicy gloss to a joint of fine Dorset lamb, and the residue in the roasting tin makes a delicious gravy. Try to use Dorset cider and honey to make this dish – Dorset has a thriving community of beekeepers, and locally produced honey is available all over the county.

> 1.5-2kg/3-4 lbs joint of Dorset spring lamb, leg or shoulder
> Salt and pepper
> 1 teaspoonful ground ginger
> 1 dessertspoonful dried rosemary
> 2 good tablespoonfuls runny honey
> 300ml/ ½ pint dry cider

Pre-heat the oven to 200ºC/400ºF/Gas Mark 6. Rub all over the lamb with the salt, pepper and ginger, then place the joint in a roasting tin or dish and sprinkle the rosemary all over it. Dribble the honey all over the lamb, and pour the cider around it.

Calculate the cooking time of the lamb, allowing 25 minutes per ½ kg (1 lb) weight of the joint, plus 20 minutes extra. Cook the lamb near the top of the pre-heated oven for 30 minutes, then baste the meat and reduce the oven temperature to 180ºC/350ºF/Gas Mark 4 for the remaining cooking time. Baste the meat every 20 minutes or so, adding a little extra cider if necessary.

When the lamb is cooked, transfer it to a warmed dish and keep hot whilst you make a gravy to accompany it, using the residue in the roasting tin. Serve with new potatoes and seasonal vegetables.

WINTERBORNE STICKLAND, ST MARY'S CHURCH c1900 W637502

RECIPE

BACON AND APPLE PUDDING

A pig was kept by many country people in the past, and bacon and ham formed the main meat part of their diet. This savoury suet pudding was made by thrifty housewives in the past as an economical way of feeding large, hungry families.

> 225g/8oz self-raising flour
> 115g/4oz shredded suet
> Salt and freshly ground black pepper
> 2 heaped tablespoonfuls of chopped fresh parsley
> 225g/8oz bacon rashers, cut into pieces
> 1 onion, peeled and finely sliced
> 2 apples, peeled, cored and sliced
> 1 dessertspoonful of chopped fresh sage leaves
> (or a teaspoonful of chopped dried sage)

Mix the flour and suet together, season with salt and pepper and stir in the chopped fresh parsley. Mix it all together with just enough cold water to form a firm dough. Knead the dough until it is smooth, then roll it out into a rectangle about 1cm (½ inch) thick. Cover the dough with the bacon pieces, then the sliced onions and apples, leaving a margin around the edge. Sprinkle with the sage, then season to taste with pepper (you should not need to add salt, as the bacon will already be salty). Dampen the edges and roll it all up like a Swiss roll. Wet the ends, and pinch them together firmly to seal them. Loosely wrap the roll in a piece of buttered, pleated greaseproof paper and then in a further piece of buttered, pleated foil (this allows room for expansion during cooking). Seal the edges and ends of the wrapping well and tie with string to secure. Half-fill a large saucepan with water and bring it to the boil. Put in the pudding, cover the pan with the lid and cook the pudding in boiling water for 2½ - 3 hours, topping up the pan with more boiling water if necessary, to ensure it does not boil dry. Serve cut into slices.

WIMBORNE, WOMEN AT THE ALMSHOUSES
1908 60634x

DORCHESTER, CORNHILL 1891 28514

RECIPE

DORSET SAUSAGE

The author Thomas Hardy, famous for his novels about Dorset life and people in the 19th century, was born in 1840 in a picturesque Dorset cottage in Higher Bockhampton, near Dorchester. Apart from five years spent in London, Hardy lived there for almost 30 years, leaving in 1874 when he married his first wife, and he wrote his first three published novels there: 'Desperate Remedies', 'Under the Greenwood Tree' and 'Far From the Madding Crowd'. The cottage, set in a pretty garden, is now in the care of the National Trust. On the outskirts of Dorchester is Max Gate, the home that he designed for himself and where he lived from 1885 until his death in 1928. Max Gate is also now in the care of the National Trust, but Hardy's study where he wrote his greatest novels, 'Tess of the D'Urbervilles' and 'Jude the Obscure', has been recreated in the Dorset County Museum in Dorchester. This recipe for Dorset Sausage is based on one that was used at Max Gate. Despite its name, this is more of a meat loaf than a sausage, and is eaten cold. This is best made the day before it is eaten.

> 450g/1 lb minced beef
> 450g/1 lb minced ham or bacon
>   (de-rinded bacon rashers can also be used)
> 225g/8oz fresh breadcrumbs
>   (from a wholemeal or granary loaf for the best results)
> A pinch of freshly grated nutmeg
> Half a teaspoonful ground mace
> 2 eggs, beaten
> Salt and pepper

Pre-heat the oven to 180°C/350°C/Gas Mark 4. Mix the meats together in a bowl, then add the breadcrumbs and mix again. Add in the beaten eggs and seasonings, and combine it all well together. Grease a 900g (2 lb) loaf tin, and fill it with the mixture. Cover the top of the tin with foil and stand it in a roasting tin filled with enough very hot water to come halfway up its sides. Bake in the pre-heated oven for 1½ hours or until the surface feels firm to the touch, topping up the tin with more hot water if necessary. Remove from the oven and leave in the tin to cool completely before turning out, preferably overnight. Cut into thick slices and serve cold.

MAIDEN NEWTON, A WAGGON 1906 54563x

RECIPE

PHEASANT WITH MUSHROOMS

You can acquire pheasant legally nowadays, but poaching game in the past was an offence punishable by transportation or hanging. There are gruesome reminders of those days in the man-traps in the Dorset County Museum in Dorchester; these vicious devices with jagged teeth that snapped shut to trap a leg were hidden by gamekeepers in undergrowth to catch trespassers in search of a pheasant or partridge for the pot.

> 1 pheasant, jointed
> 250ml/8 fl oz red wine
> 3 tablespoonfuls of oil
> 4 tablespoonfuls of sherry vinegar
>   (if hard to find, use balsamic or red wine vinegar)
> 1 onion, peeled and chopped
> 2 rashers of smoked bacon, de-rinded and cut into strips
> 350g/12oz mushrooms, sliced
> 350ml/12 fl oz chicken stock
> 1 bouquet garni
> Salt and pepper

Marinade the pheasant the day before: place the pheasant in a dish, add the wine, half the oil and half the vinegar, and half the chopped onion. Season, then cover and leave in a cool place for 8-12 hours, turning the joints from time to time to infuse the flavours.

Pre-heat the oven to 160°C/325°C/Gas Mark 3. Take the pheasant joints from the dish and pat them dry with kitchen paper, reserving the marinade. Heat the remaining oil in a large casserole dish, and brown the joints, then transfer them to a plate. Add the bacon and remaining onion to the casserole, and cook gently until the onion is soft. Add the mushrooms and continue to cook for a further 3 minutes. Stir in the remaining vinegar, and boil until it has reduced. Add the reserved marinade, the stock and the bouquet garni and cook for a few minutes. Return the pheasant to the casserole, put on the lid and cook in the pre-heated oven for about 1½ hours. When the joints are cooked, transfer them to a serving dish and keep warm. Boil the cooking juice left in the casserole dish until it has reduced and thickened slightly. Remove the bouquet garni, pour the juice over the pheasant and serve.

DORSET RABBIT

The Isle of Portland (actually a peninsula, not an island) is famous for its stone quarries that produce a fine, white stone renowned as a building material. A custom specific to Portland is that rabbits are associated with bad luck, and it is taboo to mention them by that name – they are referred to as 'underground mutton', 'long-eared furry things' or 'bunnies', but never rabbits. This derives from the quarry workers, who thought rabbits were a danger to them as their burrows caused cave-ins and rockfalls. The sight of a rabbit in a stone quarry was a bad omen, and reason to pack up tools for the day and do no further work. This superstition is still so strong on Portland, especially among the older people, that when the Wallace and Gromit film 'The Curse of the Were-Rabbit' was released in 2005, specially printed posters advertising the film had to be produced for display on Portland, with the film's title replaced with 'Something bunny is going on'. So, if you are serving this dish on Portland, you will have to call it something else!

1 jointed rabbit
25g/1oz plain flour, seasoned
115g/4oz streaky bacon rashers
150ml/ ¼ pint dry cider
115g/4oz shredded suet
225g/8oz fresh breadcrumbs
2 onions, peeled and finely chopped
Grated rind of half a lemon
1 teaspoonful dried sage
1 beaten egg
A little milk

Pre-heat the oven to 180°C/350°F/Gas Mark 4. Blanch the rabbit joints in boiling water, then pat dry. Roll the rabbit joints in the seasoned flour so that they are coated all over, then place them in a casserole dish. Lay the bacon rashers on top of the rabbit joints, and pour the cider over. Mix together the suet, breadcrumbs, grated lemon rind, dried sage and finely chopped onions. Bind the mixture together with the beaten egg and a little milk. Cover the rabbit with the topping. Cover the casserole with its lid and bake for two hours in the pre-heated oven, then remove the lid and cook for a further 20-25 minutes, so that the topping browns.

SIXPENNY HANDLEY, FROGMORE POND AND THE VICARAGE c1950
S794006

In former centuries the bounds of the Cranborne Chase in north-east Dorset stretched from Shaftesbury to Blandford and Wimborne in Dorset, Fordingbridge in Hampshire and Salisbury in Wiltshire, with the town of Cranborne as its centre. From the time of the Norman kings until 1830, the Cranborne Chase was an area reserved for deer hunting. During this period the needs of the deer dominated the area, and for fifteen days either side of Midsummer, when most of the fawns were born, the Lord of the Chase could charge 'cheminage' to all travellers through the Chase, a levy taken as compensation for the disturbance they would cause to the deer. The vast numbers of deer inevitably attracted poachers in the past, and an inscription on a gravestone in the churchyard at Sixpenny Handley on the edge of the Cranborne Chase records that poachers would leave deer carcasses in an empty tomb there until they could be disposed of in safety. Nowadays, venison in Dorset is much more easily acquired, from a number of good butchers, farm shops and farmers' markets.

RECIPE

VENISON POT ROAST

Venison is a rich, well-flavoured meat. It can sometimes be dry, but a good way of cooking it is in a pot roast or casserole, to make sure it is tender and juicy.

- 1.75kg/4-4½ lbs boned joint of venison
- 5 tablespoonfuls of oil
- 4 cloves
- 8 black peppercorns, lightly crushed
- 12 juniper berries, lightly crushed
- 250ml/8fl oz red wine
- 115g/4oz smoked streaky bacon, chopped into small pieces
- 2 onions, finely chopped
- 2 carrots, chopped
- 150g/5oz mushrooms, sliced
- 1 tablespoonful plain flour
- 250ml/8fl oz stock
- 2 tablespoonfuls redcurrant jelly
- Salt and pepper

<u>Marinade the venison the day before it is needed:</u> place the joint in a bowl, add half the oil, the spices and the wine, cover and leave in a cool place for 24 hours, turning the meat occasionally so that all sides absorb the flavour.

Pre-heat the oven to 160°C/325°F/Gas Mark 3. Remove the venison from the marinade and pat it dry with kitchen paper. Reserve the marinade to use later. Heat the remaining oil in a large shallow saucepan, and brown the venison evenly on all sides. Transfer the meat to a large casserole dish. Add the bacon, onions, carrots and mushrooms to the saucepan the venison was browned in, and cook for about 5 minutes. Stir in the flour and cook gently for 2 minutes, stirring all the time, then remove the pan from the heat and gradually stir in the marinade liquid, stock, redcurrant jelly and seasoning to taste. Return the pan to the heat and bring to the boil, stirring continually, then reduce the heat and simmer for 3 minutes. Pour the sauce into the casserole dish with the venison, cover the dish with its lid and cook in the oven for about 3 hours, until the meat is really tender. Turn the meat occasionally in the dish whilst it is cooking. Serve the venison cut into slices, with the sauce and vegetables spooned over.

DORSET CHEESES

A number of excellent cheeses are made in Dorset by artisan cheesemakers. Here are some to look out for:

Award-winning West Country Farmhouse Cheddar is made by Denhay Cheese at Broadoak, near Bridport (www.denhay.co.uk), which also produces farmhouse butter and excellent dry-cured bacon.

The Cranborne Chase Cheese Company (www.cranbornechasecheese.co.uk) near Shaftesbury makes a delicious soft white mould ripened cheese called Win Green, named after the highest point in north Dorset, as well as Wind Whistle, a semi-soft cheese with a sweet, nutty flavour; the King's Favourite, washed in cider made from the Crimson King apple; and Gold Hill, named after Shaftesbury's famous cobbled street (see page 53), a small camembert-style cheese that oozes with flavour.

The delightfully-named Windswept Cow Cheese Company at Worth Matravers on the Isle of Purbeck (www.purbeckproducts.co.uk) produces St Aldhelm Blue, a lightly veined cheese with a crumbly texture.

There are also some excellent cheeses made from goats' milk in Dorset, such as the Woolsery English Goat Cheese made at Up Sydling near Dorchester (www.woolserycheese.co.uk) and the Billie's Goat's Cheddar made by Ford Farm at Litton Cheney near Dorchester (www.fordfarm.com). Ford Farm also makes Dorset Red, a smoked cheese made from cow's milk.

But the cheese that Dorset is famous for is the moist and crumbly Blue Vinney, the classic blue veined hard cheese referred to by William Barnes in the poem on page 2. According to tradition, the cheese was made on farms in the old days by immersing old harnesses or shoes in the milk, where bacteria present on the leather encouraged the blue mould to develop! Dorset Blue Vinny (without an 'e') cheese is now produced by modern hygienic processes on Woodbridge Farm at Stock Gaylard near Sturminster Newton (www.dorsetblue.com), which is also the home of the Dorset Blue Soup Company.

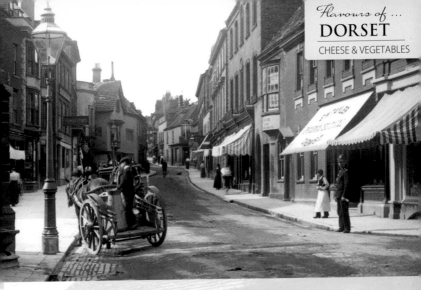

SHERBORNE, A MILK CART IN CHEAP STREET 1903 49719x

DORSET KNOBS

An important cottage industry of Dorset in the past was button making. For about two hundred years from the late 1600s many women in the county made their living working from home at 'buttony', covering thin rings of sheep's horn or wire rings with pieces of linen and then stitching them in a variety of patterns and styles, with names like Dorset High Top, Blandford Cartwheel and Dorset Knob. The name of the Dorset Knob button is recalled in a Dorset speciality, the light, crisp roll-shaped Dorset Knob biscuits produced by the Moores bakery in west Dorset (www.moores-biscuits.co.uk). They are about the size of a golf ball, with a rusk-like texture, and are ideal for eating with cheese. However, there is a knack to splitting open a Dorset Knob so that it can be spread with butter or cheese, without this brittle delicacy exploding into pieces. The trick is to insert the point of a sharp knife into its side, and then twist it – the Knob should then split into two pieces.

Flavours of ...
DORSET
CHEESE & VEGETABLES

RECIPE

BLUE VINNY AND WATERCRESS FLAN

Use Dorset watercress and Blue Vinny cheese to make this savoury flan if possible. If you can't get Blue Vinny, use another hard blue cheese, such as Stilton or Shropshire Blue.

175g/6oz plain flour
75g/3oz butter or margarine
Salt and freshly ground black pepper
150g/5oz Dorset Blue Vinny cheese, rinded and cut into thin slices
3 eggs, beaten
300ml/ ½ pint fresh milk
1 medium onion, peeled and finely chopped
75g/3oz fresh watercress (trimmed weight),
       with the thick stalks trimmed off

Pre-heat the oven to 200°F/400°F/Gas Mark 6. Grease a flan dish or tin about 20-24cms (8-9 inches) in diameter. Sift the flour into a mixing bowl with the salt, and rub in the butter or margarine. Add just enough cold water to mix it together to form a firm dough, and knead lightly until it is smooth and elastic. Roll out the dough and use it to line the flan tin. Place a piece of greaseproof paper with some baking beans on the pastry base and bake it blind for 10 minutes, then remove the beans and paper and cook for a further 5 minutes to dry out the base. Remove from the oven, and reduce the oven temperature to 190°C/375°F/Gas Mark 5.

Place the slices of cheese (and any crumbs) over the pastry base. Mix together the beaten eggs, the milk and the chopped onion, and season to taste with freshly ground black pepper but only a little salt, if needed, as the cheese will already contain some salt. Roughly chop the trimmed watercress and stir it into the egg mixture, combine it well, then pour it into the pastry case. Bake in the oven at the reduced temperature for 40-45 minutes, until the flan is cooked but not dry, and the filling is risen and firm to the touch. This should not be eaten hot straight from the oven, but leave it to cool a little and eat it warm, or otherwise eat it cold.

UPWEY, THE WISHING WELL c1897 34554a

RECIPE

CABBAGE AND POTATO PIE

A variety of cultivated cabbage is said to have been have been introduced to England by Sir Anthony Ashley, who imported cabbage seed from Holland in the 16th century to grow cabbages in the kitchen garden of his house at Wimborne St Giles in Dorset. A comment in a gardener's book of 1699 reads: 'Tis scarce 100 years since we had Cabbages out of Holland. Sir Arthur Ashley, of Wilburg St Giles in Dorsetshire, being the first who planted them in England.' Sir Anthony Ashley died in 1628 and his magnificent Jacobean tomb in the village church shows a facetted spherical object at the foot of his effigy which some sources claim is a heraldic representation of a cabbage; sadly this is not true – the object depicts a polyhedron, and was probably put there as a mark of Sir Ashley's status as an educated man with an interest in science and geometry.

> 450g/1 lb potatoes
> 450g/1 lb cabbage
> 2 onions, peeled and thinly sliced
> 25g/1oz butter
> A little milk
> A pinch of salt
> Freshly ground black pepper
> 115g/4oz cheese, grated

Oven temperature: 190°C/375°F/Gas Mark 5.

Boil the potatoes until they are very soft, then mash them with butter and a little milk. Season with salt and pepper. Boil or steam the cabbage until it is tender. Mix together the mashed potato, cabbage and onion slices, and turn into a greased pie dish. Sprinkle the grated cheese on to the top of the pie, and bake in a pre-heated oven for 20-30 minutes, until the top has browned.

**CHARMOUTH
BOYS AND A CART
1890** 27382x

39

RECIPE

ROASTED PUMPKIN

The beautiful Purbeck region of east Dorset is famous for its stone quarries, and also for the ruined castle that looms spectacularly over the picturesque village of Corfe Castle. South of Corfe on the Purbeck coast is Worth Matravers, where every October local people gather at the Square & Compass pub for an annual pumpkin festival. Pumpkins, squashes and gourds in a variety of shapes, sizes and colours are on display, and stalls sell all sorts of produce made from pumpkins. The highlight of the day is the weigh-in, overseen by a compére dressed in full pumpkin costume, when the heaviest monster vegetable is declared the festival's champion. You won't need a giant pumpkin for this recipe though! Pumpkin is probably best known for making a wonderful soup, but it also makes a delicious vegetable dish with a sweet flavour when simply roasted in the oven like this. Serves 4-6.

    1 medium pumpkin, about 24cms (6-9 inches) in diameter
    3 tablespoonfuls olive oil
    A handful of fresh sage leaves (left whole, not chopped)
    Salt and freshly ground black pepper
    Half a teaspoonful freshly grated nutmeg

Pre-heat the oven to 200°C/400°F/Gas Mark 6.

Peel the pumpkin, de-seed it and cut the flesh into chunks or slices about 4cm (1½ inches) thick. Put the pumpkin pieces into a large roasting tin with 2 tablespoonfuls of the olive oil, season with salt and pepper, and toss the pieces in the oil so that all the sides are coated. Roast the pumpkin in the pre-heated oven for 35-40 minutes, or until the pieces are golden and tender when tested with a skewer or the point of a sharp knife, turning them once during the cooking time. Add the sage leaves to the tin for the last 5 minutes of the cooking time. Remove the tin from the oven, drizzle the rest of the olive oil over the pumpkin pieces and grate a little nutmeg over them. Serve straight away.

Flavours of ...
DORSET
CHEESE & VEGETABLES

CORFE CASTLE, THE VILLAGE AND THE CASTLE
c1955 C160015

RECIPE

MOONSHINE

This version of bread and butter pudding was called Moonshine in
several old recipe books from Dorset.

> 50g/2oz butter
> 6 thin slices of white bread, with the crusts removed
> 50g/2oz sultanas
> 50g/2oz caster sugar
> 400ml/ ¾ pint milk
> 150ml/ ¼ pint single cream
> 3 eggs
> Grated rind of half a lemon
> Freshly grated nutmeg

Use some of the butter to grease a shallow ovenproof dish. Use the
rest of the butter to spread on the bread slices. Cut the bread into
strips and arrange in layers in the dish, buttered side up, sprinkling
each layer with sultanas and sugar, finishing with a layer of buttered
bread.

Pre-heat the oven to 180°C/350°F/Gas Mark 4.

Break the eggs into a bowl and beat. Heat the milk and cream to just
below boiling point, then pour it onto the eggs, stirring all the time.
Add the lemon rind. Pour the mixture over the bread in the dish,
sprinkle the top with grated nutmeg. Allow to stand for 30 minutes,
then bake in the pre-heated oven for 35-40 minutes, until the custard
is set and the top is crisp.

RECIPE

BLACKBERRY SYLLABUB

Wild blackberries grow all over Dorset's countryside, festooning hedgerows with delicious fruit. They are ripe from early August until late September, and have a much better flavour than the commercially grown blackberries available in supermarkets – and it's much more fun to go out in the countryside foraging for them. If you can stop yourself eating them all, some of the blackberries you collect can be frozen to be used out of season. This quick and easy recipe makes a delicious dessert, and can be made a few hours before serving if necessary. Serves 6.

300g/10oz blackberries
75g/3oz caster sugar (or a little more if you wish)
300ml/10 fl oz/ ½ pint double cream
Finely grated zest and juice of half a lemon
2 tablespoonfuls dry white wine (optional)

Reserve 6 of the blackberries for decoration, then use a potato masher or suchlike to crush the rest of the berries with the lemon zest and 50g/2oz of the sugar, until you have a gooey, runny mush. In separate bowl, whip together the cream, the lemon juice and the remaining sugar, gradually adding in the wine (if using) when the mixture is beginning to thicken. Carry on whipping until soft peaks form, and the mixture is thick and light, but not stiff. Gently fold the cream mixture into the blackberry mush, using a large metal spoon, leaving a rippled effect.

Divide the mixture between 6 glass dessert dishes, and top each serving with one of the reserved blackberries. Either serve immediately, or cover the glasses with cling film and store the desserts in the fridge until needed.

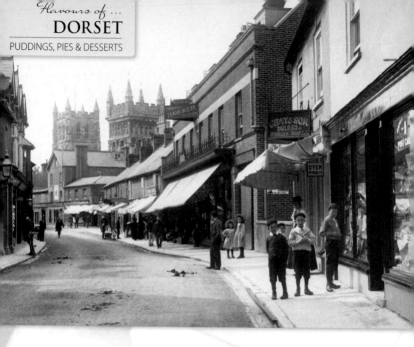

WIMBORNE, EAST STREET 1904 52475

A well-known name in Dorset is that of The Dorset Blueberry
Company of Hampreston, near Wimborne, where the light and
acidic sandy soil is particularly suited to blueberry cultivation. The
company, run by the Trehane family, has been growing blueberries
commercially for many years now and is the UK's leading producer of
organically-grown blueberries. Most of its crop goes to supply Marks
& Spencer and other outlets, but the company runs a Pick-Your-Own
operation from the farm and also sells its fruit and a wide range of
blueberry products at a number of farmers' markets, both in Dorset
and further away, including Borough Market in London. For details of
where they have a stall, see the Events section of their website: www.
trehane.co.uk

RECIPE

BLUEBERRY AND ALMOND FLAN

This is not a traditional Dorset recipe, but almonds have been used in English cookery since medieval times, and feature in many dishes in old Dorset recipe books. Blueberries go particularly well with almonds, which seem to intensify their delicious flavour. The layer of jam at the bottom helps to seal the pastry base and prevent it going soggy.

> 225g/8oz shortcrust pastry (made with 225g/8oz plain flour,
>   and 115g/4oz butter or margarine)
> 150g/5oz blueberries
> 115g/4oz butter, softened to room temperature
> 115g/4oz caster sugar
> 2 eggs, beaten
> 115g/4oz ground almonds
> Half a teaspoonful almond essence
> 1 tablespoonful jam, blueberry if possible,
>   but any flavour can be used

Pre-heat the oven to 200ºC/400ºF/Gas Mark 6 and place a baking tray in the oven to heat up. Grease a flan dish or tin about 20-24cms (8-9 inches) in diameter. Roll out the pastry and use it to line the flan dish. Beat the butter and sugar together until light and fluffy. Gradually beat in the eggs, a little at a time, adding some of the ground almonds if necessary to prevent the mixture curdling, then mix in all the ground almonds and the almond essence. Spread the jam over the bottom of the pastry case, and then the blueberries. Cover with the almond mixture, and spread it gently all over to form an even surface. Place the flan dish on the baking tray in the preheated oven (this helps the pastry base to cook through properly) and bake for 10 minutes, then reduce the oven temperature to 160°C/300°F/Gas Mark 3 and bake for a further 20-25 minutes, until the filling is slightly risen and golden brown, and feels firm to the touch. Remove from the oven and leave to cool before serving. Can be eaten warm or cold.

BLANDFORD FORUM, THE MARKET PLACE c1900 B28230I

Blandford Forum in north Dorset is renowned as the best and most complete Georgian town in England, as it was rebuilt following a fire that devastated the town in 1731 to a comprehensive design for the whole project that was overseen by the Blandford architect brothers, John and William Bastard. This photograph shows the remarkable Georgian market place that was devised and built between 1733 and 1739. The impressive building on the right hand side of this view is the Corn Exchange, where local farmers came on Market Day to sell their produce to the merchants, who had stands in the Exchange. The recipe for Blandford Apple Pudding on the opposite page is a modern adaptation from a recipe book of the early 1800s from Blandford St Mary, just outside the town, now in the Dorset Record Office (reference D176/25). Although it is called a pudding, it is really more of a tart or flan, with a filling made from apple purée thickened with eggs. It is best to prepare the apple pulp by baking the apples in the oven, rather than stewing them in water, as it results in a drier pulp and gives a much better result.

RECIPE

BLANDFORD APPLE PUDDING

For the pastry:
175g/6oz plain flour
A pinch of salt
75g/3oz butter or margarine

For the filling:
450g/1 lb cooking apples
3 eggs
50g/2oz butter
75g/3oz caster sugar
Grated zest of half an orange
A pinch of freshly grated nutmeg

Heat the oven to 200°C/400°F/Gas Mark 6. Grease a flan dish or tin about 20-24cms (8-9 inches) in diameter. Use a sharp knife to score a line around the outside of each apple. Remove the cores from the apples with an apple corer, but do not peel them. Stand the apples in an ovenproof dish, add 2 tablespoonfuls of water to the dish and bake in the pre-heated oven for 40 minutes until the apples are tender. Whilst the apples are baking, make the pastry and cook the pastry case. Sift the flour into a mixing bowl with the salt, and rub in the butter or margarine. Add just enough cold water to mix it into a firm dough, and knead lightly until it is smooth and elastic. Roll out the dough and use it to line the flan tin. Prick the pastry all over with a fork to allow air bubbles to escape during cooking. Place a piece of greaseproof paper with some baking beans on the pastry base and bake it blind in the hot oven for 10 minutes, then take out of the oven and remove the beans and paper. When the apples are cooked, reduce the oven temperature to 180°C/350°F/Gas Mark 4.

Scrape out the pulp from the cooked apples, and push it through a sieve, to remove any small pieces of skin and form a purée. Melt the butter in a saucepan, then leave to cool for a few minutes. Use a balloon whisk to beat together the eggs and sugar, then stir in the apple pulp. Beat in the orange zest, the grated nutmeg and the melted butter, and mix it all together well. Pour the mixture into the pastry case and bake in the oven at the reduced temperature for 20-25 minutes, until the filling is risen and firm to the touch. Remove from the oven and leave to cool a little before eating, when the filling will thicken and firm up. This can be eaten warm or cold.

EYPE, JESSAMINE COTTAGE 1897 40089

Apples feature in many old recipes from Dorset and were grown in great numbers in the county in the past. In 1815 William Stevenson wrote in his 'General View of the Agriculture of the County of Dorset' that 'there are upwards of 10,000 acres of orchard ground'. Dorset Apple Cake was officially voted Dorset's National Dish in 2006, yet there does not seem to be a definitive recipe. Some people make it with spices, some without. Some people include dried fruit, others prefer it without. Traditionally, cooking apples seem to have been used, but it can be made with dessert apples if necessary. The earliest apple cake made in the poorest kitchens was just a bread dough with pieces of apple kneaded into it, before eggs, sugar and spices became cheap enough for more than just the rich to afford, and that was probably the version referred to by Reverend William Barnes in his Dorset dialect poem 'Father Come Home' of 1835:

> *'He's nice an' moist; vor when I were-a meakin on,*
> *I stuck some bits ov apple in the dough.'*

170°F

RECIPE

DORSET APPLE CAKE

225g/8oz self-raising flour
1 heaped teaspoonful baking powder
115g/4oz butter or margarine
A pinch of salt
225g/8oz prepared weight of apples, peeled,
    cored and chopped into small pieces
115g/4oz soft brown or caster sugar
1 egg
1 dessertspoonful milk
50g/2oz raisins or sultanas (optional)
A pinch of cinnamon or mixed spice (optional)
A little extra sugar to sprinkle on top

Pre-heat the oven to 190°C/375°F/Gas Mark 5 (slightly less for a fan oven) and grease and line a 20-24cm (8-9 inch) round cake tin.

Sift the flour, baking powder and salt into a bowl. Rub in the butter or margarine until the mixture resembles breadcrumbs. Add the chopped apple pieces to the mixture, and then add the sugar and the dried fruit and spice (if using). Beat the egg with the milk, and add to the mixture. Mix it all together well, to form a firm dough – it will seem quite stiff, but this is how it is meant to be, as the apples will cook down to form a moist cake. Turn the mixture into the prepared cake tin, smooth the top and sprinkle the top with sugar. Bake just below the centre of the pre-heated oven for about 45 minutes, until the top of the cake is golden brown and firm when you gently press down on it.

Leave to cool in the tin for 15 minutes, then turn out the cake on to a wire rack. This can be eaten either hot or cold, perhaps with the slices split open and spread with butter. It also makes a delicious pudding, served hot with cream, custard or ice-cream. If eating as a cake, leave on the wire rack to cool completely, and store in an airtight tin.

RECIPE

MATRIMONY CAKE

The most usual recipe for Matrimony Cake is for a date slice made with oats and flour, or breadcrumbs, symbolising that you take the rough with the smooth in a marriage. This alternative version for a sweet, spicy layer of apples and currants between two layers of pastry is an old recipe that was popular in various parts of England in the past, including Dorset. There was a tradition in some parts of the country for it to be served at wedding feasts, cut into as many pieces as there were guests present – hence its name of Matrimony Cake.

> 225g/8oz shortcrust pastry (made with 225g/8oz plain flour, and 115g/4oz butter or margarine)
> 50g/2oz fresh brown breadcrumbs
> 4 large cooking apples, peeled, cored and sliced into thin rings
> 50g/2oz currants or raisins, or a mixture of both.
> Half a teaspoonful ground nutmeg and ground ginger, mixed
> Juice of half a lemon, and one thick slice of lemon
> 50g/2oz caster sugar
> 2 tablespoonfuls golden syrup
> A little milk to glaze the pastry

Pre-heat the oven to 180°C/350°F/Gas Mark 4. Grease a flan or baking tin 20-24cm (8-9 inch) round or square. Roll out half the pastry and use it to line the tin, including the sides. Arrange the apple rings in an overlapping layer on the pastry base. Cover the apples with the dried fruit, filling the core holes, then add the breadcrumbs, sugar and golden syrup, and sprinkle the nutmeg, ginger and lemon juice evenly over the filling. Place the lemon slice in the middle of the mixture. Dampen the edge of the pastry. Roll out the remaining pastry to form a lid and lay it on top of the cake, pressing the edges very firmly together to seal them. Trim off any excess pastry, brush the pastry with a little milk, and bake in the pre-heated oven for about 30 minutes, until the pastry is crisp and golden. This is usually served hot, with cream.

DORCHESTER, A COUPLE 1913 65618v

RECIPE

BLACKMORE VALE CAKE

The Blackmore Vale is part of the valley of the River Stour, which flows into the Vale north of Gillingham and out at Blandford Forum. The Vale is bounded by the chalk ridge of the Dorset Downs to the south, the chalk hills of the Cranborne Chase to the east and northeast, and the watershed between the valleys of the Rivers Stour and Yeo to the northwest. A wonderful vista of the Blackmore Vale can be enjoyed from the hilltop town of Shaftesbury, perched on an escarpment on the northern edge of the Vale and famous for its picturesque cobbled street of Gold Hill, which featured in a well-known TV commercial for Hovis bread. This is an old recipe from the area, traditionally associated with the Blackmore Vale Hunt. It is a fruit cake with a dense texture rather like gingerbread. It would originally have been made with black treacle, which gives a darker cake and a good flavour, but golden syrup can be used if preferred.

> 115g/4oz butter, softened to room temperature
> 115g/4oz caster sugar
> 150ml/ ¼ pint milk
> 1 tablespoonful black treacle or golden syrup
> 1 teaspoonful bicarbonate of soda
> 350g/12oz plain flour
> 350g/12oz raisins
> 50g/2oz mixed chopped candied peel

Pre-heat the oven to 160°C/325°F/Gas Mark 3. Grease and line a 20-24cm (8-9 inch) round cake tin. Cream together the sugar and the butter until light and fluffy. Warm the milk to hand-hot, add the black treacle or golden syrup and allow it to dissolve in the milk, then add the bicarbonate of soda. Gradually add the sieved flour to the creamed butter and sugar, alternating it with a little of the milk and treacle mixture, and beating it well after each addition. Mix in the raisins and candied peel and combine it all thoroughly. Turn the mixture into the prepared cake tin, level the top and bake just below the centre of the pre-heated oven for about 2 hours, until the top feels firm to the touch when gently pressed. Cover the top of the cake with foil towards the end of the cooking time if it seems to be browning too quickly.

SHAFTESBURY, GOLD HILL c1955 S593056

FRANCIS FRITH

PIONEER VICTORIAN PHOTOGRAPHER

Francis Frith, founder of the world-famous photographic archive, was a complex and multi-talented man. A devout Quaker and a highly successful Victorian businessman, he was philosophical by nature and pioneering in outlook. By 1855 he had already established a wholesale grocery business in Liverpool, and sold it for the astonishing sum of £200,000, which is the equivalent today of over £15,000,000. Now in his thirties, and captivated by the new science of photography, Frith set out on a series of pioneering journeys up the Nile and to the Near East.

INTRIGUE AND EXPLORATION

He was the first photographer to venture beyond the sixth cataract of the Nile. Africa was still the mysterious 'Dark Continent', and Stanley and Livingstone's historic meeting was a decade into the future. The conditions for picture taking confound belief. He laboured for hours in his wicker dark-room in the sweltering heat of the desert, while the volatile chemicals fizzed dangerously in their trays. Back in London he exhibited his photographs and was 'rapturously cheered' by members of the Royal Society. His reputation as a photographer was made overnight.

VENTURE OF A LIFE-TIME

By the 1870s the railways had threaded their way across the country, and Bank Holidays and half-day Saturdays had been made obligatory by Act of Parliament. All of a sudden the working man and his family were able to enjoy days out, take holidays, and see a little more of the world.

With typical business acumen, Francis Frith foresaw that these new tourists would enjoy having souvenirs to commemorate their days out. For the next thirty years he travelled the country by train and by pony and trap, producing fine photographs of seaside resorts and beauty spots that were keenly bought by millions of Victorians. These prints were painstakingly pasted into family albums and pored over during the dark nights of winter, rekindling precious memories of summer excursions. Frith's studio was soon supplying retail shops all over the country, and by 1890 F Frith & Co had become the greatest specialist photographic publishing company in the world, with over 2,000 sales outlets, and pioneered the picture postcard.

FRANCIS FRITH'S LEGACY

Francis Frith had died in 1898 at his villa in Cannes, his great project still growing. By 1970 the archive he created contained over a third of a million pictures showing 7,000 British towns and villages.

Frith's legacy to us today is of immense significance and value, for the magnificent archive of evocative photographs he created provides a unique record of change in the cities, towns and villages throughout Britain over a century and more. Frith and his fellow studio photographers revisited locations many times down the years to update their views, compiling for us an enthralling and colourful pageant of British life and character.

We are fortunate that Frith was dedicated to recording the minutiae of everyday life. For it is this sheer wealth of visual data, the painstaking chronicle of changes in dress, transport, street layouts, buildings, housing and landscape that captivates us so much today, offering us a powerful link with the past and with the lives of our ancestors.

Computers have now made it possible for Frith's many thousands of images to be accessed almost instantly. The archive offers every one of us an opportunity to examine the places where we and our families have lived and worked down the years. Its images, depicting our shared past, are now bringing pleasure and enlightenment to millions around the world a century and more after his death.

For further information visit: www.francisfrith.com

INTERIOR DECORATION

Frith's photographs can be seen framed and as giant wall murals in thousands of pubs, restaurants, hotels, banks, retail stores and other public buildings throughout Britain. These provide interesting and attractive décor, generating strong local interest and acting as a powerful reminder of gentler days in our increasingly busy and frenetic world.

FRITH PRODUCTS

All Frith photographs are available as prints and posters in a variety of different sizes and styles. In the UK we also offer a range of other gift and stationery products illustrated with Frith photographs, although many of these are not available for delivery outside the UK – see our web site for more information on the products available for delivery in your country.

THE INTERNET

Over 100,000 photographs of Britain can be viewed and purchased on the Frith web site. The web site also includes memories and reminiscences contributed by our customers, who have personal knowledge of localities and of the people and properties depicted in Frith photographs. If you wish to learn more about a specific town or village you may find these reminiscences fascinating to browse. Why not add your own comments if you think they would be of interest to others? See **www.francisfrith.com**

PLEASE HELP US BRING FRITH'S PHOTOGRAPHS TO LIFE

Our authors do their best to recount the history of the places they write about. They give insights into how particular towns and villages developed, they describe the architecture of streets and buildings, and they discuss the lives of famous people who lived there. But however knowledgeable our authors are, the story they tell is necessarily incomplete.

Frith's photographs are so much more than plain historical documents. They are living proofs of the flow of human life down the generations. They show real people at real moments in history; and each of those people is the son or daughter of someone, the brother or sister, aunt or uncle, grandfather or grandmother of someone else. All of them lived, worked and played in the streets depicted in Frith's photographs.

We would be grateful if you would give us your insights into the places shown in our photographs: the streets and buildings, the shops, businesses and industries. Post your memories of life in those streets on the Frith website: what it was like growing up there, who ran the local shop and what shopping was like years ago; if your workplace is shown tell us about your working day and what the building is used for now. Read other visitors' memories and reconnect with your shared local history and heritage. With your help more and more Frith photographs can be brought to life, and vital memories preserved for posterity, and for the benefit of historians in the future.

Wherever possible, we will try to include some of your comments in future editions of our books. Moreover, if you spot errors in dates, titles or other facts, please let us know, because our archive records are not always completely accurate—they rely on 140 years of human endeavour and hand-compiled records. You can email us using the contact form on the website.

Thank you!

For further information, trade, or author enquiries
please contact us at the address below:

**The Francis Frith Collection, Oakley Business Park,
Wylye Road, Dinton, Wiltshire SP3 5EU.**
Tel: +44 (0)1722 716 376 Fax: +44 (0)1722 716 881
e-mail: sales@francisfrith.co.uk **www.francisfrith.com**